What makes the wind blow?

come from?

What is a virus?

WHAT MAKES YOU GROW?

DON'T PEOPLE FALL OFF IT?

WHAT TURNS MILK SOUR?

What makes a match light?

WHAT MAKES A BALL BOUNCE?

WHY DOES IT SNOW?

WHAT DO SHOTS DO FOR YOU?

WHERE WAS THE SUN ALL NIGHT?

How does television work?

WHY IS THERE SAND ON THE BEACH?

How is ice cream made?

★THE QUESTION AND ANSWER BOOK★

RANDOM HOUSE

★OF EVERYDAY SCIENCE★

HOW DOES WATER PUT OUT FIRE?

The
QUESTION
and
ANSWER

Book of Everyday Science

by
Ruth A. Sonneborn

Illustrated by
Robert J. Lee

Random House · New York

To Jill, who will soon be
asking these questions, with a special
nod of thanks to her grandfather

CONTENTS

QUESTIONS AND
ANSWERS
ABOUT

The Sky and the Outdoors   9

Water   17

Fire and Heat   21

Your Body   27

Food You Eat   35

Things You Use   45

Machines that Work for You   61

INDEX OF SUBJECTS   69

About the Sky and the Outdoors

Why is the sky blue?

What we call the sky is nothing but air with billions of tiny dust particles floating in it. It gets its blue color from the sun.

The light from the sun is a mixture of violet, blue, green, yellow, orange and red rays. But we never see these colors separately except when they appear to us in a rainbow. The red-orange-yellow rays of light stream straight down to earth from the sun. But the violet-blue-green rays are different. They are scattered by the tiny dust particles in the air. When we look up we see the blue light rays reflected by the dust particles. We see the blue sky.

Where was the sun all night?

The sun was in the sky where it always is. It's you, your spot on the earth, that turned away from the sun. Our big round earth keeps spinning all the time. Sometimes the place where you live is turned toward the sun. Then it's day for you. Sometimes the place where you live is turned away from the sun. Then, because there is no sunlight, it's night for you.

There is always day somewhere in the world and always night somewhere else. Daytime, nighttime, brightness, darkness, our world turns around every twenty-four hours bringing night and day over and over again to you and to all people on our earth.

**If the earth is round,
why don't people fall off it?**

What keeps you on the round earth as it travels and spins? And why does the ball you toss up in the air fall down? And why, when you jump, do you go up just a little way and then come right back down? It's because the earth pulls you, pulls your ball, pulls everything to it. This strong pull of the earth—and it is very, very strong — we call gravity. Gravity holds us all on the earth. It holds us so fast that we never need to worry about falling off.

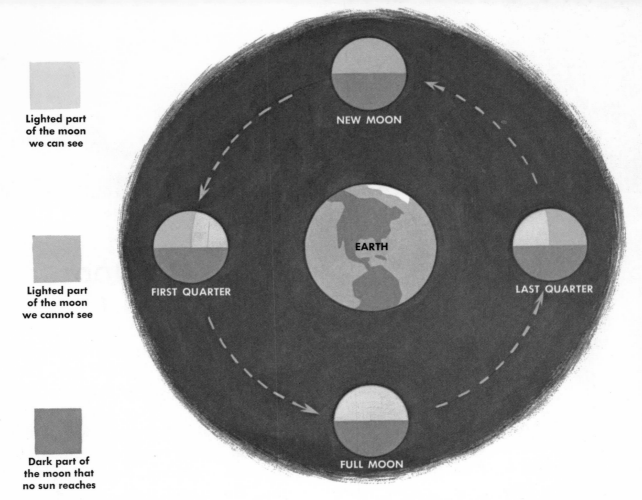

Lighted part of the moon we can see

Lighted part of the moon we cannot see

Dark part of the moon that no sun reaches

NEW MOON

EARTH

FIRST QUARTER

LAST QUARTER

FULL MOON

Why does the moon look sometimes big, sometimes small?

The moon has no light of its own. Light comes to it from the sun just as light comes to our earth. A part of the moon is always turned to the sun and a part of it is always turned away from the sun. One part is dark as night. The other part is bright as day. We see the moon only when some of the lighted part is turned toward the earth. Then the moon is catching light from the sun and throwing it down to earth. We call this light reflected light.

The moon keeps traveling in space around the earth. It makes one whole circle in about a month. As the moon travels around the earth, it seems to change its shape. Sometimes we see only a thin sliver. The sun is lighting up one whole side of the moon, but only a thin curved edge of this lighted part is turned toward us. The next night, as the moon moves around us, we see more of the lighted part. Night by night we see more and more until finally we see the whole round, shining face of the moon.

The moon keeps on moving around us and now each night we see less and less of it. Then one night we see no moon at all. The moon is now between the earth and the sun. The sun is not shining on the side turned to us. The moon's dark face is turned toward us. But soon again we will see a thin sliver of moon up in the sky. Once more we will watch it grow bigger and smaller.

What are the stars?

The stars are great balls of hot, glowing gases, whirling and whirling and whirling in space. They are suns pouring out light just as *our* sun does. They look tiny to us but really they are very big. Many of them are much bigger than our sun. They look smaller because they are so far away. They are much farther away even than our sun. And our sun is ninety-three million miles away!

It's hard to believe that the tiny pinpoint of starlight you see up there in the night sky is a gigantic sun, isn't it? And do you know there are about 2,500 stars you can see in the sky at one time without using a telescope, and many millions more you can see with the help of a powerful telescope?

Why is your shadow sometimes tall, sometimes short?

Light cannot shine through you. Your body blocks it. There is a dark spot in front of you that the light cannot reach. This is your shadow. The length of this shadow depends on where the light comes from.

When you stand out under the noonday sun, the sun is almost directly overhead. The light streams down on the top of your head, the top of your shoulders and your feet. You stop very little light from reaching the ground, and so your shadow is very little.

But when you are out in the early morning or late afternoon, the sun is low in the sky. The light streams over the full length of your body—from head to feet. Then a long, long shadow stretches out there on the ground, for your body is keeping a great deal of light from reaching the ground.

What makes clouds?

Those beautiful white clouds are little droplets of water surrounding tiny bits of dust so small you cannot see them. How did they get up there in the sky?

When the sun shines down hot, it heats the water on our earth. It heats the water in lakes, in brooks, in rivers, in puddles, in oceans. The heat changes the water on the surface to vapor. The water vapor mixes with the light warm air and with it is pushed upward by the heavy cold air. Cold air is always dropping down and pushing light warm air up and up. The vapor rises higher and higher until finally it begins to cool. When the vapor grows cool, it is changed back into tiny drops of water.

Specks of dust have also been carried up by the warm air. The dust and the drops of water meet and cling together up in the sky. So when you look up you see a beautiful white cloud sailing along.

What makes it rain?

Those gray and black clouds in the sky are clouds that are very full of water. There are many more droplets of water crowded into them than into white clouds. The droplets are cold and heavy. The air all around them is warmer and lighter. And so they begin to fall. Down, down, down they come.

As they fall they meet and mix with other droplets. They grow bigger. Soon big drops of rain spatter down on our earth, into lakes and rivers and the ocean, onto fields and houses and streets. Someday the drops of water will once again become clouds. From earth to sky and from sky to earth, water keeps changing to vapor and vapor to water.

What makes the colors in the rainbow?

Sunlight may look yellow or white to you. But it is really violet and blue and green and yellow and orange and red. When all these colors are mixed together they make a bright white. But when the light rays from the sun stream down through drops of rain, something happens.

The drops of water separate the colors. And if you stand so that the sun is behind you and the rain is falling in front of you, the rays of the sun will pass into the raindrops and you will see a band of violet, blue, green, yellow, orange and red across the sky. In this rainbow you will see all the separate colors that make up sunlight. To see a rainbow you must have both rain and sunshine.

What makes thunder and lightning?

Lightning is really just a huge electrical spark. In the winter, if you scuff your feet on a wool rug and then touch a metal lamp, there will be a tiny spark. This spark, in its small way, is like lightning. And it is caused by electricity.

All storm clouds or thunderclouds contain a kind of electricity. Sometimes when they are very full of this electricity it flashes out like a giant spark and leaps from cloud to cloud. Or sometimes it strikes the earth, doing great damage. That giant spark is lightning, and as it travels it heats the air in its path. The sudden heating of the air makes it spread out, makes it expand. As the heated air expands it bumps into layers of cool air. This bump or collision sets up a great air wave. It rolls around in the sky, and we hear thunder.

14

What makes the wind blow?

Wind is just air moving, and it is differences in temperature that make the air move. Hot air is thinner and lighter than cold air. You can't see that it is thinner or feel that it is lighter, but people have discovered this difference by studying the air with special instruments.

When heavy cold air meets light hot air, the cold air drops down and pushes the hot air up out of its way. The air starts moving, a little breeze begins to blow. The air over the earth is cool in some places, hot in others. Over lakes and forests it is cool. Over city pavements and deserts it is hot. When large areas of hot air meet large areas of cold air, then big winds begin to blow.

Over the desert hot air rises; over the

Why is the grass wet in the early morning?

All day long the grass is dry and warm. The sun has made it so. Then the sun goes. And when the sun goes the warmth goes. The grass grows cold. The air touches the cold grass and leaves little beads of water on it.

All air has water vapor in it. Warm air can hold more of this water vapor than cold air. So when the night air is cooled by the grass, it can no longer hold all its water vapor. The water clings to the grass, forming dew. The dew will stay there until the sun rises high in the sky. Then the heat of the sun will change the little beads of water into vapor, and the grass will grow warm and dry again.

snowy peaks the cold air drops down.

Why does it snow?

When it's very cold—freezing cold—up in the clouds, the water vapor is changed into tiny bits of ice. These tiny bits are crystals. The crystals grow and some cluster. Then they begin to fall. They are beautiful snowflakes, each one a different lovely shape.

Though they look so light and airy, the snowflakes are too heavy to stay in the cloud, too heavy for the warmer air beneath the cloud. Down they tumble, twirling and drifting to our earth. If the earth is warm, they will touch it and change into drops of water. But if the earth is cold, they will stay snowflakes and gently cover everything with their whiteness.

15

What holds an island up?

An island looks as though it is floating on top of the water. But if you took a shovel and began to dig, you would dig and dig and never get to the bottom. Islands are really mountains. Most of the mountain is under water. Just the top is out in the air. That is the part you see. Sometimes islands disappear when waters rise high, and sometimes new islands appear when waters drop. But all of these islands are part of the surface of the earth, part of its wrinkly crust. They are not floating on top of the water.

Why is there sand on the beach?

The ocean water makes the sandy beach. As the busy pounding waves bound into the shore, they crush the pebbles, rocks and shells. They carry the pieces out and then in again. Out and in. The waves keep crushing the pebbles, rocks and shells, grinding them together until they are tiny bits or particles of sand.

Rivers and streams grind up rocks and pebbles, too. They carry them down to the ocean. Then the waves pile all the sand up on the shore, so there is a soft, sandy beach for you to play on.

About Water

Why is the water in the ocean salty?

There is salt in the soil, in rocks, in the earth. When the ocean waves lick at the shore they collect salt. And when the rivers run into the ocean, they bring salt with them from rocks and from the earth. All this salt stays in the ocean. Fresh clean rain falls into brooks, rivers, reservoirs. It makes the water you drink taste sweet. But the rain cannot make the ocean water taste sweet. The ocean is too big and too full of salt.

Why does an iced-drink glass "sweat"?

You pick up your cold drink. The glass feels cold and the outside of it is wet. You can easily understand that the coldness of your drink makes the glass cold. But what makes the glass "sweat"? Why is it wet?

The air around your cold glass is warm. Like all air there is water in it. You can't see this water because it's a vapor. But the minute the vapor touches your cold glass, it turns to water that you can see. The tiny beads of water cling to your glass. And this is the "sweat" you see and feel.

Why does ice float?

The ice cubes at the bottom of your glass pop right up to the top when you pour in water. What makes them do that?

Something happens to water when it turns to ice. The ice takes up more room than it did as water. It spreads out, expands. This makes the ice cubes lighter than the water, so they float.

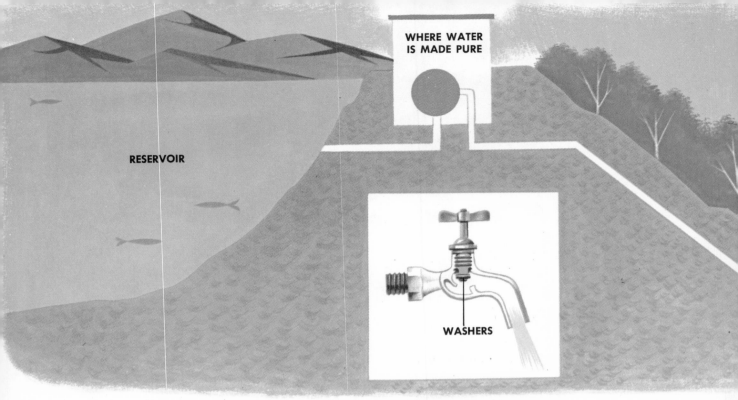

WHERE WATER IS MADE PURE

RESERVOIR

WASHERS

Where does your water come from?

If you live in the city your water comes to you from a big water storage place called a reservoir. The water in the reservoir is collected from rivers and brooks, from rain and snow. It is stored there and made pure and clean. Then pipes carry it to you. They run under the street and you can see them only when a repair crew comes to fix a leak.

But if you live in the country the chances are that your water comes from your own private storage place, your own well. Somebody dug this well for you. He dug deep down in the earth until he reached water. Then he built a leak-proof place to catch and store this water. Pipes bring it to your house.

Water from the surface of the earth for city people; water from deep down in the earth for country people. We get our water wherever we find it most easily.

How does the water get to your faucet?

If you live in the country and get your water from a well, a pump does the work of pushing the water through a pipe to your faucet. Water from deep down in the earth needs a big push to get up to your faucet.

But if you live in the city and get your water from a reservoir, it usually runs right to your house without any help. This is because water can climb to the same height it started from. Since much of the water in cities comes from reservoirs high in the mountains, it can run up that high again. If your water supply comes from the top of a really high mountain, it can run up to a faucet on the nineteenth or twentieth floor of a city building.

But if the reservoir is in a low place the water may have to be pushed through the pipes by a pump.

How does your faucet
turn the water on and off?

You can see only the handle of your faucet. You can't see the short metal rod that runs down to the water pipe. The bottom of this rod is wrapped around with rubber rings, called washers. These rubber washers act as a stopper. When the faucet is turned off, the stopper closes the pipe and keeps the water from flowing out the spout or spigot. But if you turn the faucet on, you pull the stopper away from the pipe.

Turn the faucet just a little and there will be only a small opening in the pipe. You will get just a trickle of water. Turn it all the way and you will open the pipe completely. There will be a rush of water. Now turn the handle of your faucet back again, as far as it will go. No more water can flow out, for the faucet is turned off. You have pushed the stopper back into the pipe.

Why doesn't hot water
get mixed up with cold water?

A big pipe brings the water from outside into your house. It brings in cold water. Inside your house the big pipe branches out into two smaller pipes. Cold water flows along in one of these pipes straight to your cold water faucet. And cold water flows along in the other pipe to your hot-water heater. Here it is heated until it is hot, and then a pipe carries it along to your hot-water faucet.

When you turn on this faucet you get hot water. The hot and cold water can't mix unless you turn on both faucets at the same time and mix them yourself.

Where does your bath water go?

You pull the stopper out of your bathtub and the water gurgles away down the drain. Your drain opens into a special pipe. This pipe was built to carry away dirty water, to keep it from mixing with clean water.

In the country a drain pipe usually carries the water off underground. In the city, drain pipes from houses are joined to big sewer pipes under the streets. The dirty water flows through the sewers—sometimes for miles and miles—to an ocean, a river, a deep underground pool, a storage tank. It flows through filters that clean it. But no matter where it goes, you can be sure that the dirty water will not be allowed to mix with the clean, pure water you drink, cook with and bathe in.

Why do you see your breath on a cold day?

You breathe out into cold, frosty air, and there's your breath—a thin, white mist floating before your face. But on a hot day you can't see your breath. Why?

The warm, moist air from your lungs has water in it. It is vapor. In summer your warm, moist breath mixes with the warm, moist air around you. You cannot tell the difference between your breath and the air. But it's different on a cold day. Vapor changes to water when it gets cold. And so the cold air changes your warm, moist breath into a stream of tiny droplets of water. It is those tiny droplets that you see.

Why do windows steam up?

When you take a hot bath the bathroom window gets especially steamy, doesn't it? And the kitchen window clouds up when there is a pot cooking on the stove.

The air in both these rooms is very hot and wet. When the wet hot air touches the cold window pane, it cools very quickly. Cool air cannot hold as much water as hot air, and so tiny droplets of water are left clinging to the window. We say that the window is steamy.

About Fire and Heat

What makes a match light?

You rub the tip of the match against a rough patch and it flames at once. Whenever two things are rubbed together they get hot. But some things can be rubbed together for a long time without flaming. They will get hot but they will not burn. The tip of your match has been dipped into a chemical. This chemical needs only a little heat to make it burn. You don't have to scratch the match more than once or twice before it lights.

How does water put out fire?

You watch a fire. You see the bright flames leap up in the air. Without that air all around it, your fire would die out quickly. Air has something called oxygen in it. And whatever you use to make your fire — wood, paper, coal — needs to mix with oxygen in order to burn. When you pour water on the fire, you keep away most of the air. Without oxygen the flames die down. At the same time water cools the burning wood or coal. They cannot burn if they are not hot.

You've probably noticed what happens if you put a wet log on the fire. It doesn't really burn. It steams, it smokes. But as soon as the log dries out, the air mixes with it. The log grows hot and begins to burn.

Why does smoke go up?

The gray smoke from the fire is a stream of tiny specks of ash, wood or paper that the flames have not been able to burn up. The smoke-filled air over the fire is very, very hot. Farther away from the flames the air is colder. Since cold air is heavier than hot air, the hot smoky air cannot hold up the heavy cold air above it. This cold air drops down, pushing the hot air up out of its way.

Hot smoky air is so very light that a small push will send it floating up and up and up until you can no longer see it.

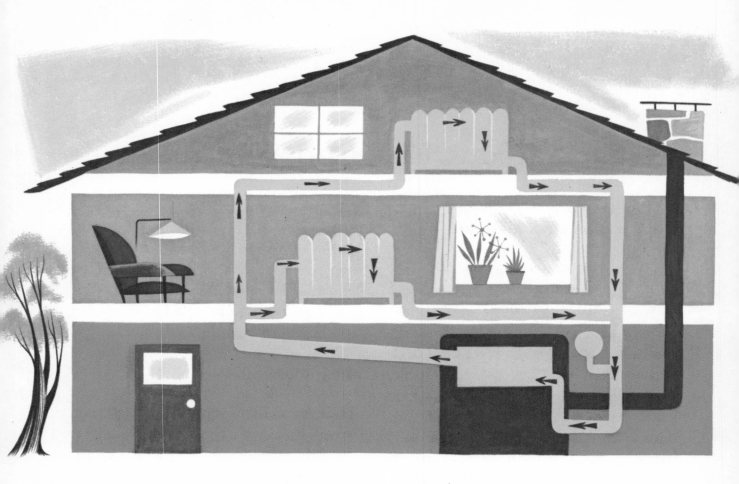

The rooms in this house are heated by radiators. Hot water or steam is forced through pipes to the radiators. By following the arrows, you can trace the path of the hot water or steam as it passes through the radiators, cools off, and is carried back to the boiler to be reheated.

How does a furnace keep a house warm?

You know it's the fire in the furnace—burning coal, or oil, or gas—that warms your house. But how does the heat get from the furnace to all the rooms?

There are several different ways. Take a look at the room you are in and see which way is your way. Do you have open grates or registers on the floor? Then your furnace is heating your house with warm air. It heats the air trapped inside it. A blower blows it out. Hot air always rises, pushed by the heavier cold air that moves in to take its place. So the hot air from the furnace is pushed up and up through the open grates. The hot air fills your rooms and warms them.

Or are there pipes and radiators in

your rooms? If there are, your furnace is heating water to warm your house. Your furnace is connected to a boiler filled with water. When the water is very hot, a pump pumps it up a pipe to your radiators.

Or the water may be boiling hot and become steam. Steam takes up more room than it did as water. And so it is forced through the pipes to your radiators. The heat from the hot water or the steam travels right through your metal radiators out into your room. When the water cools off or when the steam turns back into water, it is carried back down to the boiler to be reheated.

But whether your heat is coming by way of hot air, hot water or hot steam, that fire in the furnace is really doing the job.

Where does gas come from?

The blue flame under the pot on your stove may be burning gas that comes from just around the corner or from hundreds of miles away. It may be gas that was made in a huge furnace. Or it may be natural gas that was made in the earth.

Men drill to find natural gas. They find it deep down in pockets underground. There it formed and was trapped by layers of rocks years and years ago. Huge pipes are laid into the gas pockets to carry the gas away. The pipes run for hundreds and hundreds of miles—often over many states. Smaller

The drill goes through many layers of earth to find gas.

pipes branch out to towns and cities on the way. And from big storage tanks the gas is piped out to streets, to homes, to stoves.

But how do we get the other kind of gas, the gas made in big gas plants? This gas is made from coal. The coal is dropped through chutes into a special kind of tank. The tank is closed up tight to keep the air out. Without air the coal will not burn. This is important because the coal must be heated but it must not burn.

The heat works on the coal, breaks it up. Some of the coal stays solid, some of it becomes liquid and some of it turns to vapor. It is the vapor, cooled and cleaned, that is the gas you cook on. It will be piped to your house or delivered to you in tanks. It will make a hot blue flame and cook your dinner quickly.

How does gas give heat?

When your stove is turned on, gas flows out of the burner into the air. The heat from a match, or from the pilot light on the stove, makes both gas and air grow hot. The hot gas combines with something in the hot air called oxygen. It bursts into flame and burns. And so you have heat to cook on. Gas is a particularly good fuel for a stove because it gives steady heat, and because it is so clean.

When the flame is blue, the gas is burning up completely. But when the flame has yellow in it, you will find soot on the pot. This means that some specks such as coal dust have stayed in the gas. These specks are not burning up completely. When gas burns with a clear blue flame, it will give a steady, clean flow of heat.

Why does heat crack a glass?

You quickly pour something very hot into a glass. The glass cracks. Why?

Heat makes almost everything spread out, or expand. The hot liquid you pour into the glass heats the inside at once. But the outside is still cold. The hot inside stretches and pushes. The cold outside doesn't. It holds fast and your glass cracks. But if you pour in your liquid very, very slowly you give the glass a chance to get hot both inside and outside. It won't crack.

Of course if the glass is very thin, like the glass of an electric light bulb, it won't crack either. This is because the heat warms the inside and outside at the same time. And they spread out together.

24

How does a silver spoon stop a glass from cracking?

A glass may crack if you pour a hot drink into it quickly. The sudden heat makes it crack. But if you can let a glass warm up slowly, it won't crack. And that's just what a silver spoon does. It keeps the heat from reaching the glass quickly.

Heat travels through all metals fast, but it travels fastest through silver. When you put the spoon into a glass and then pour in a hot drink, the heat rushes into the spoon and flows up through it. Much less heat flows to the glass. The glass warms up little by little and it doesn't crack.

Why does the spoon in your soup bowl get hot?

You leave your spoon in your hot soup. When you pick it up, you drop it quickly. It's as hot as your soup. This is because your spoon is made of metal. Heat travels through metal quickly. The heat from the soup flows from the tip of the spoon up to the handle and to your hand.

Can you see now why so many kitchen things like spoons and pots don't have metal handles? They have wooden or plastic handles. Heat cannot travel fast through either plastic or wood. And that makes both of them very useful materials for the kitchen.

Why are most cooking pots made of metal?

Your mother puts a metal pot on the hot stove. What happens? Does the pot burn up? Does it crack or melt? No, it does none of those things. A very, very hot fire could melt the metal, but the fire we cook over never gets that hot. The heat from the burner flows up into the metal pot. The pot gets hot, and the heat from it flows into the food. The food gets hot and cooks. Metal is fine for cooking-pots because the heat of the stove does not destroy it, and because heat travels quickly through it.

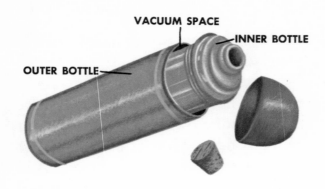

VACUUM SPACE

INNER BOTTLE

OUTER BOTTLE

How do things stay hot in a thermos?

The soup or the cocoa your mother poured into your thermos hours ago comes out steaming hot. What kept it hot? The answer is a funny one. *Nothing* kept it hot. Let's explain what we mean by that word *nothing*.

Your thermos is really two bottles, a smaller one set inside a bigger one. They are fastened together only at the top. Everywhere else there is a space between them. The air has been pumped out of this space. It's what we call a vacuum, an airless space. We can say there is really *nothing* between the two bottles.

If your hot soup or cocoa is in the inside bottle, there is *nothing* for the heat to pass through to the outer bottle. Heat must travel through something and in the airless space there is *nothing* for it to travel through. So the heat stays in your soup, in your cocoa, and you have a fine hot drink.

How do clothes keep you warm?

Of course your heavy jacket, your woolen gloves and your thick cap keep the cold air from reaching you. But that's only a small part of how they keep you warm.

Your body is always manufacturing heat. Between your body and your clothes there is always warm air. Thick woolen cloth, fur and leather are full of tiny air spaces. The air trapped in these spaces does not let heat travel through easily. So the heat which your body is always manufacturing stays between your body and your clothing. This is really how your clothing keeps you warm.

What makes the bubbles in boiling water?

It's steam—little pockets of steam—that makes the bubbles in a pot of boiling water. The hottest water in the pot is at the bottom, closest to the heat. When it gets boiling hot, the water at the bottom turns to steam and rises to the top of the pot in bubbles. The steam then escapes from the bubbles into the air. Bubbling water is water with steam popping out of it.

About Your Body

What makes you grow?

Your body is made up of millions of cells. They are so tiny that you can see them only through a microscope. But every part of you—your bones, your skin, your heart, your lungs and your muscles—is made of cells. Like you your cells are alive. And like you they need food if they are to keep alive. The food you eat feeds them. They absorb it and grow bigger. They grow bigger and then each cell divides and becomes two cells.

Two cells take up more room than one cell. And four cells will take up more room than two cells. You can easily see how the growing number of cells in the bones of your legs make your legs grow longer and thicker.

Cells have another job to do. All through your life some cells are dying and others are taking their place. When you are young this happens slowly. With older people it happens fast. When you are full grown, your cells will be busy replacing themselves. They will no longer make you grow. Lucky, isn't it? Otherwise the world would be full of giants.

How does what you eat make you strong?

The food you eat does a lot of traveling and changing from the time you put it into your mouth until the time it becomes a part of your body. You bite into a piece of steak or cake. Your teeth grind it up smaller. Then special juices in your mouth and in your stomach make these bits still smaller. They dissolve them. Finally your food is a fluid.

And all this time the food is moving.

What cells look like under a microscope.

It moves from your mouth to your stomach, then through the long coiled tubes of your intestines. As a liquid it can pass through the walls of the cells and nourish them. They grow bigger. They divide. New cells are added to your body, and some of them replace old cells. In this way your muscles and bones are kept healthy, and they grow longer and stronger.

How does your body know what to do?

You get an idea that you want to jump. Your legs bend, and you jump. You get an idea that there is something sharp in your shoe. You take it off and search. How did your arms and legs, your eyes, your whole body know what to do?

Inside your body you have a network of nerves. These nerves are like fine, thin strings that connect every part of your body with your brain. Over them messages are constantly flowing in both directions. It was your brain that sent out the jump message to your legs. And think of how many things happened to make you take off your shoe.

The nerves in your foot carried messages of pain up to your brain. Your brain sent out messages to your eyes, your hands, your back, your arms—to every part of your body—telling each part what to do. You can see what a busy place your brain is with incoming and outgoing messages and orders day and night.

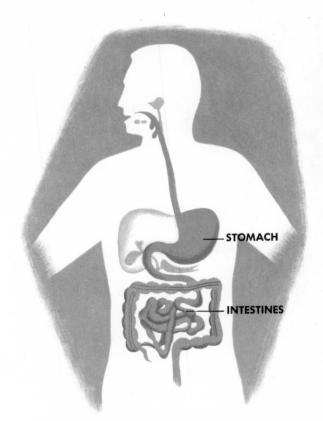

Digestive system

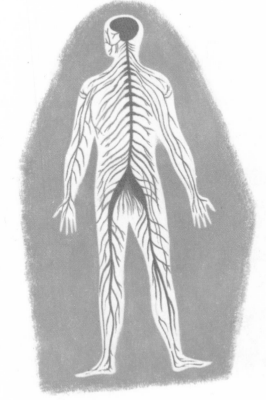

Nervous system

Why doesn't it hurt when you cut your nails or hair?

The nerves in your body are what make you feel pain. A great network of these nerves runs through your body and carries all sense of feeling to your brain. The nerves in your skin carry news about everything you touch and everything that touches you. Cold and hot, wet and dry, rough and smooth, comfortable and painful—your nerves let your brain know about all these things.

But your nails and your hair have no nerves. They are not made of flesh and blood and nerves like your skin. And so with no nerves to carry any messages from them to your brain, you don't feel anything when you cut your nails or your hair.

Why do you get hot when you run?

Perhaps you've sometimes wondered why your skin feels warm. It's your warm red blood flowing through the skin that makes it warm, that makes you warm. And it's your heart pumping night and day that keeps the blood flowing through you.

When you are quiet, your heart beats regularly and slowly. It sends out an even, slow stream of blood to your skin. But when you run fast, your heart has to beat faster. It beats faster and it sends out blood more quickly to your skin. This makes your skin warmer. Your skin feels hot. And so, of course, do you.

How does a scab form when you cut yourself?

You cut yourself and blood flows out of the cut. But soon it stops flowing. And soon you see a crust, a scab over it. What makes this scab?

There is something in your blood that mixes with a fluid in the torn edges of your skin. Together they manufacture a sticky substance that dries and hardens in the air. This is the scab. And this is how your blood closes the door after itself. It stops itself from flowing and at the same time covers the cut, protecting it from germs in the air. The scab will stay there until new skin has grown underneath it. Then when it is no longer needed, it will dry up, loosen and fall off.

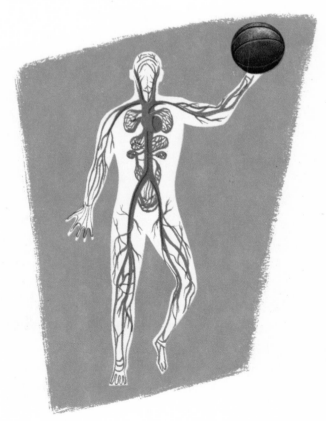

29

Circulatory system

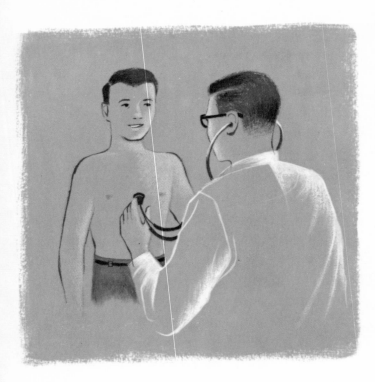

What are cavities in your teeth?

You know that cavities are holes, and that when they grow deep you get a toothache. You also know that before that happens you had better hurry off to your dentist. But how do you get a cavity?

Your teeth are very sharp and strong. They have to be to grind up your food into small bits for you to swallow. It is the outer covering on your teeth that makes them strong and keeps them strong. This hard outer layer is called enamel. Underneath the enamel the tooth is made of softer stuff.

Sometimes decaying food destroys the enamel, making a hole in it. Foods like candy and soda pop with lots of sugar in them are especially harmful. This is a chemical action that dentists and doctors still have not learned how to stop. They can only advise you to brush your teeth thoroughly and often, and to visit your dentist regularly for checkups.

Why does your doctor use a stethoscope?

Your doctor doesn't need a stethoscope just to hear your heart beating, for your heart makes a noisy thumping sound. And he doesn't need a stethoscope to hear your lungs draw in air and send it out. He uses the stethoscope so that he can hear clearly the noises in every little separate part of your heart and lungs. He can hear how each inch is working.

The end of the stethoscope he places on your chest picks up sounds from just the spot where he places it. And these sounds are carried straight to the plugs in his ears. With his stethoscope your doctor can hear clearly the tiny sounds he never would be able to hear without it.

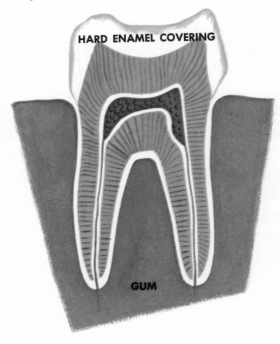

HARD ENAMEL COVERING

GUM

Why do our eyes blink?

Your eyelids blink regularly all day long. They stop only when you sleep. You can make them blink, but they don't need your help. They will keep on blinking without your thinking or even knowing about it. Blinking protects your delicate eyes from injury. Have you noticed how quickly you blink when something flies toward you? Usually your lids shut in time to protect your eyes.

Blinking also does a kind of washing job. It helps keep your eyelids moist. That's important because when a speck of dirt gets past your lids it will be trapped by your moist eyeball. Then your eye will begin to water, your lid will blink, and the speck will be washed away.

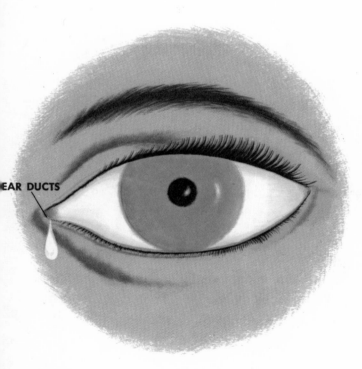

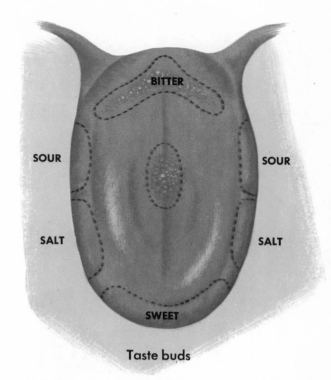

Taste buds

How are we able to taste things?

Perhaps you think that you taste food only with your mouth. But that isn't so. Your nose plays an important part. Do you remember how very little flavor your dinner had when you had a cold in the nose? That was because your sense of smell was not working.

In your mouth it is your tongue that does your tasting. Your tongue has special cells that do this. They are called taste buds. Strangely enough they bring you only four different kinds of taste—sweet, sour, salty, bitter. But with the help of your sense of smell, you are able to taste many different flavors. Chocolate, roast beef, oranges, and onions all taste very different. Your sense of smell and your sense of taste combine to let you know that each food has a special taste.

31

What makes you get goose flesh?

Suddenly you feel very cold, or something frightens you. You get goose flesh. If you look very closely you see that the hairs on your arm are standing on end. The flesh around each hair has popped up with it. A gland inside your body makes a tiny muscle push up the hair and the skin around it. Your skin looks as if it is covered by small pimples.

Nobody is sure just why this happens. Some scientists think that it is a way your skin tries to keep out the cold. And others think that goose flesh is a leftover, now-useless way man had of protecting himself. Perhaps his hair bristled just as a frightened cat's fur puffs out to make the cat look bigger and fiercer to the enemy.

Why can't babies walk?

Did you ever wonder what holds you straight when you walk? It's your bones, your straight, strong bones, isn't it? A baby's bones aren't strong like yours. His bones are rubbery. But as he grows older his bones become tough and strong. Pretty soon his backbone is firm enough so that he can sit up. And then his leg bones grow hard enough to hold up the weight of his whole small body.

He still has to learn how to use his muscles to move his legs, how to keep his balance. When he is about a year old, his bones are strong enough. And what is wonderful is that then he wants to learn how to walk. And he walks!

Why do people get freckles?

Everybody's skin has some color. It would be strange to see a chalk-white person, wouldn't it? In the skin there are some special cells that manufacture color. If your skin has many of these evenly spaced, it will be evenly colored. But if you have only a few of these cells scattered unevenly around, you will get spots of color. You will get freckles. Sunshine makes these cells work faster. That's why some people get so brown out in the sun and other people get so many freckles.

What is a germ?

When we hear the word *germ*, we usually think of harmful disease germs. These are tiny living things, so small that we cannot see them without a microscope.

If these disease germs get into our bodies they may cause harm to our cells. One germ can grow into millions of

What is a virus?

Viruses are the cause of many diseases, but they are much tinier than most of the disease germs described above. In fact many viruses are so small that you can't see them through an ordinary microscope. You must have a very special instrument, an electron microscope, to see them.

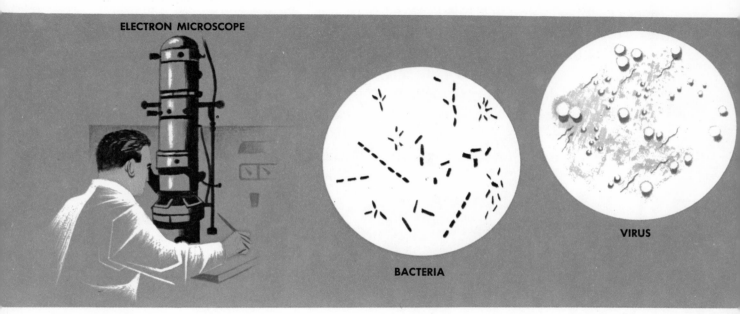

ELECTRON MICROSCOPE

BACTERIA

VIRUS

germs very rapidly. Harmful germs can give us a cough or make a scraped knee swell up with pus. They may give us a fever or a case of measles.

But there are also useful germs. One of them turns milk into cheese; another turns sweet fruit into vinegar. Germs are everywhere around us and in us. We can protect ourselves from the germs that make us sick by keeping our bodies clean and strong.

But doctors usually know when viruses are present even if they can't see them. When you get polio, measles or mumps, the doctor knows there are viruses at work in your blood stream. They grow rapidly. One virus can become many viruses faster than you can count. Doctors are learning each day how to protect you from more of these viruses. Perhaps someday they'll be able to protect you from all of them.

What do shots do for you?

Your doctor gives you shots to keep you well and protect you from harmful illnesses such as polio and diphtheria. But exactly what is a shot and how does it work?

When the doctor gives you a polio shot, he shoots a very small number of weakened or dead polio viruses into your blood stream. At once your blood starts to fight these viruses. It makes something, a chemical substance, that destroys the viruses. And you do not get sick.

This wonderful chemical substance stays in your blood ready to fight and destroy any really strong polio viruses that may later get into your blood. From time to time the doctor will give you more shots, booster shots, to make sure that your blood always has the power to fight these viruses.

But when your doctor gives you a diphtheria shot, he doesn't shoot weakened or dead diphtheria germs into your blood stream. Instead he injects into you something called a serum. This serum is distributed by drug companies. It is the same thing your own blood would have to make if you had diphtheria. And one shot of it keeps you from getting diphtheria.

Why do you have to get vaccinated?

You get vaccinated so that you will never catch smallpox. Years ago many people died of smallpox. If they didn't die, their faces were usually left pitted and scarred from the disease.

Nowadays almost no one gets smallpox because almost everyone is vaccinated. When your doctor vaccinates you, he is really giving you a very, very light case of smallpox. It's so light that only your vaccination mark shows you have had it. He presses the needle against your skin, forcing in a few dead or very weakened smallpox viruses.

As soon as these viruses get into your blood stream, your blood fights them. It destroys the viruses and also makes something that will stay in your blood and fight any smallpox viruses that may come your way later. This substance will stay in your blood for about seven years. And then your doctor should vaccinate you again.

About Food You Eat

Where does pepper come from?

The spicy black pepper that many people like to sprinkle on their food comes from the berries of pepper plants. These pepper plants grow in warm countries in the Far East—India, Malaya, and their neighbors. There the farmers plant pepper plants in long rows.

The plants grow and climb up poles the way beans do. After a while clusters of green berries appear. These berries are about the size of peas. When they turn yellow—before they are red and ripe—the berries are picked. Then they are dried in the hot sun or before a slow fire.

Now the little dried pepper berries are ready for cooks who like to use them whole. But for people who like to sprinkle pepper on their food, the little black berries must be ground fine and put in shaker containers.

Where does salt come from?

Salt is almost everywhere in the earth. It's in the soil, in the rocks, in the ocean, even in lakes and rivers. It is scattered everywhere, but in some places the salt collects in a mass. A mass of salt may be imbedded in a rock, a patch of ground that was once the bottom of a salty lake, or in an underground pool.

When men find this salt, they mine it or pump it up. Then they cart it to a salt factory—a salt refinery is the correct name. There the freshly mined salt is dumped into a big vat full of water which is heated very hot. The water boils and steams. It steams away out of the vat until there is no more water left in the vat. At the bottom the salt crystals lie sparkling. These salt crystals are filtered, washed clean and packaged in the round boxes you buy. The clean white salt will make your food taste good.

Where does chocolate come from?

Chocolate comes from a tree, but it's not called a chocolate tree. It's called a cacao. That's where we get the word cocoa. The cacao tree grows in very hot countries and produces the seed or bean from which all chocolate comes. The small

seeds or beans grow inside a pod that is much larger than our pea pods. When the pods look fat and ripe, men cut them off the tree. They spread them out in the hot sun to dry. The dry pods can be easily shelled.

After the chocolate beans have been dried still more and roasted in a machine, they travel on a moving belt between rollers. These rollers crush and grind the beans to a fine powder. Then more rollers grind and rub the powder until it melts into a dark brown liquid. It looks like chocolate syrup, but you wouldn't like the taste of it. It's very bitter. The candy or syrup factory will put in the sugar that makes it taste sweet and good.

How is flour made?

The soft, white powdery flour your mother keeps in the kitchen was once part of a tall golden grass. It is made from the grain or seed of wheat. How did this tough little wheat seed become a soft white powder?

In the old days people used to grind the grain between two flat stones to get rid of the tough skin and to crush the soft inside kernel. This was long and hard work. Today many machines speed through the job. Huge rollers crush the grain. Huge sifters separate the tough outside from the soft kernels. Other machines grind the kernels into a powder. The powder is forced through silk cloth to make it still finer. And then it is cleaned and bleached white by blasts of air.

Soft, white powdery flour is now ready for you, but just think of all the machines that helped make it.

How is bread made?

Who makes most of the bread eaten to-day? Machines do. Modern bakeries boast that no human hands ever touch your bread until you do. Instead, many, many machines do the work.

The first machine is something like a huge electric mixing bowl. It is called a hopper. Sifted flour is piped into the hopper and there mixed with yeast and warm water. When the mixture pops out of the hopper, it is a huge ball of dough. Now it is wheeled into a warm, damp room. In this room something very important happens. Here the yeast makes gas bubbles and the bubbles push around inside the dough. They make it spread out. They make it rise.

Now the dough, puffier than before, is wheeled to a machine and mixed with other things—salt to make it taste good, vitamins to make it good for you. Then the dough makes a second trip to the warm damp room, where it will rise still more.

Next, two machines divide and shape the dough into loaves. And now after a third trip to the warm, damp room the dough is ready for baking. It glides on a moving belt through huge ovens, where men check it by peeping through small windows. At the end of the trip, it emerges. It is cooled, sliced and wrapped by machines. And there is your bread, ready for you to eat.

Cutting the sugar cane

Sugar mill or refinery

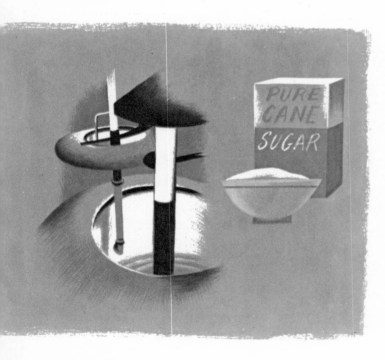

Whirling machine that separates raw sugar

Where does sugar come from?

Most of our sugar comes from the juice of a plant called sugar cane. It grows under a very hot, hot sun. Long rows of sugar cane stretch out for miles on big plantations. The plants grow tall, taller than a man. When they are ripe workers come with sharp knives. With one slash they strip off the leaves. The bare stalks are then rushed to a nearby sugar mill. There they are dumped onto a moving belt and pressed flat between heavy rollers. The sweet juice is squeezed out, and flows down into tanks below.

Next the juice is strained and boiled. It becomes a dark brown molasses in which sugar crystals are floating. To remove the molasses the mixture is poured into a whirling machine. The rapid whirling flings out the molasses and leaves the brown sugar crystals at the bottom. This is raw sugar. The raw sugar goes to a sugar refinery to be melted, purified, dried, sifted and ground fine. And now it is the white sparkling kind of sugar you sprinkle on your cereal.

How does milk get from the cow to us?

Did you ever stop to think how much traveling milk does before it gets to your table? Every day the farmer milks his cows twice. Every day he pours the milk into big milk cans, cools it, and sets the cans alongside the road. And every day along comes a milk tank truck. The driver pumps or pours the milk from the cans into the tank. The tank is a huge thermos, so it keeps the milk cold on its way to the dairy plant.

In the dairy the milk is pumped into big tanks. Electric motors whirl huge blades that separate the cream out of the milk. Pipes carry the milk to a machine to purify it. Here the milk is heated enough to kill any disease germs that may be in it. Now pipes carry the milk to a bottling machine. And then it is ready for its last trip in a refrigerated truck or train. Each morning it arrives fresh at your neighborhood store.

How is butter made?

Did you ever whip cream too long, for-getting to stop when it was whipped enough for the top of your chocolate pudding? If you did, you ended up not with whipped cream but with butter. That's almost the way butter is made in big white dairy buildings all over the country. Fresh cream is pumped into a big tank and heated enough to kill any harmful bacteria or germs that may be in it.

After the cream has been cooled, it goes to the "whipping tank." This is called a churn. Huge beaters driven by an electric motor whip or churn the cream. After a while, if you could peek inside the churn, you would see little yellow blobs about the size of a pea floating in a white liquid. These are bits of butter floating in butter milk.

The butter milk is drawn off and the bits of butter are washed and churned some more. Then big scrapers scrape the butter out of the tank and push it into molds. It is left to harden. And now, after it has been wrapped and packaged, the butter goes to your store. It is ready for your piece of bread.

What makes a cake in the oven fluff up?

When you put the uncooked cake batter in the oven to bake, it fills just a little part of the pan. But when you take it out, you have a high, fluffy cake that fills the pan. How does this happen?

You do a lot of beating with an egg beater or an electric beater when you mix the batter. You force air into the batter. You can see the air bubbles, can't you? In the batter there is something else that makes bubbles. That's baking powder. A chemical in the baking pow-der mixes with the milk or water and makes gas bubbles. As the cake bakes in the hot oven, the air bubbles and gas bubbles spread out. They push the batter up. The batter rises, and when your cake is finished it is high, fluffy and light.

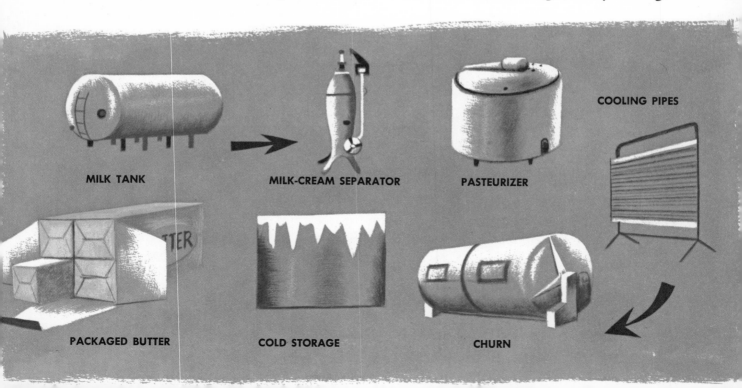

MILK TANK

MILK-CREAM SEPARATOR

PASTEURIZER

COOLING PIPES

PACKAGED BUTTER

COLD STORAGE

CHURN

THE FREEZING ROOM

How is ice cream made?

A very important man in an ice-cream plant is the mix-man. Can you guess why he's called that? First he sees to it that the right amount of cream, milk, sugar — everything but the special flavoring — is put into the mix. The mix is stirred into a big vat. It is cooked and purified by high heat. Then it flows through big cooling pipes, pipes colder than your refrigerator. These pipes freeze the mix very fast. If they didn't it would not freeze smoothly.

Now the mix is ready for a flavor. The mix-man puts chocolate in some and strawberry, vanilla, maple — dozens of different kinds of delicious flavors — in others. Each flavor of mix then is forced through its own cooling pipe, to its own freezing tank. Here paddles beat air into it to make it smoother and lighter. It is now ready to be packaged or stored in a huge refrigerator. It is ice cream — delicious, flavory ice cream ready for you to spoon up in a dish or lick in a cone.

What thickens gelatin?

You pour the tiny, bright grains of gelatin into a bowl. You add warm water and the grains mix with the water. Now there is a colored liquid in your bowl.

These are all changes you can see, but you can't see what happens when the liquid cools. You can't see the grains of gelatin change to tiny filmy bits. And you can't see these tiny filmy bits surround droplets of the liquid. They surround these droplets, holding them inside. Then the filmy bits move close together. They cling to one another. And when this happens your gelatin has jelled!

41

Why doesn't food spoil in a can?

Inside a can the food is protected from the things that would make it spoil. What are these things? Bacteria, the tiny little living plants that are everywhere around us. Bacteria, sometimes called germs, are so tiny that we can see them only under a microscope. But they are powerful.

Like all living things, bacteria need food to grow. When they grow they multiply. A few bacteria become many in a matter of minutes. When bacteria settle on food, they make changes in it. These changes are what we call spoiling.

To keep food from spoiling, we must first kill any bacteria that may already be in it. Heat and cooking do this. Next we must keep any bacteria in the air away from the food. So we pack it into cans as airless as we can make them. We seal the cans tight. With no bacteria in the food and no air with bacteria able to reach it, fruit, fish, meat and vegetables will stay unspoiled in a can for years.

How is food kept fresh when it's shipped far away?

When food is shipped, it is kept fresh in exactly the same way your mother keeps food fresh for you. She keeps it in the refrigerator, doesn't she? Well, today most foods are sent on long journeys in huge refrigerators. Trains carry refrigerator cars for meats, vegetables and fruits. Engines pull refrigerator tanks carrying fresh milk. Trucks are built with bodies that are refrigerators on wheels. And even cargo planes have sections with built-in refrigerators.

Like your home refrigerator, these all make ice and keep things cold with the help of electricity. All kinds of fresh food can now travel from any part of the world to us. And they arrive tasting almost as though they had been raised on the nearest farm.

Why are foods frozen?

They are frozen to check the enemy, the tiny little living plants called bacteria that spoil food. Bacteria are found in food, in the air, everywhere. When they find something to eat, they settle on it. They eat, grow bigger, split in two. And these two bacteria go on to become four, eight, sixteen, hundreds. They spoil our food, making it unfit for us to eat.

But we have learned how to fight bacteria. One of the best ways is to freeze them. Bacteria cannot grow in the cold. And so we can fill our freezers full of fresh food that will stay fresh for us as long as it stays frozen.

How are foods frozen?

Did you know that we got the modern idea for quick freezing of foods from the Eskimos? In their natural "ice freezers" they sometimes keep food for years. When explorers and hunters first tasted the frozen food of the Eskimos, they were surprised to find how fresh it was. Now we copy the Eskimos.

Vegetables, fruit, fish, meat must all be prepared for freezing. All are cleaned and some are cooked. Then machines package them in boxes and containers. After that they are ready to be placed in freezers which freeze them very quickly. They must be frozen quickly to keep their fresh taste. You can thank the Eskimos the next time your mother serves you fresh-tasting strawberries on a cold winter day.

How do worms get inside apples?

The worm you find in your apple was born there. It has lived all its life there. But it is still a baby. The curious thing is that when it grows up it will no longer be a worm. It will be an insect with wings.

In the spring insects bore tiny holes in the small green apples and lay eggs in the holes. After a while worms hatch from these eggs. They live in the apple and feast on it. Then when the apples fall to the ground, the worms squirm out. They cover themselves with a hard skin and bury themselves in the ground.

The following spring, the hard skin cracks open and out comes an insect— the same kind of insect as the one that laid the eggs inside the apple. And this insect may very well lay eggs inside another apple, from which still more worms will hatch.

What makes a banana turn black, an apple turn brown?

Just as chemical action makes bananas and apples grow big and ripe, it also makes them turn black or brown. Fruit, like plants and animals, is made up of cells. These cells grow. The fruit grows. Chemical action is at work. Finally the fruit is full-grown and ripe. The cells stop growing.

But the chemical action doesn't stop. It now begins to change the cells, to destroy them. They become soft and mushy. And when air reaches the soft spots, it works along with the chemical action. Dark spots appear on the fruit. It is overripe.

What turns milk sour?

Perhaps you never thought of milk as a sweet drink. But really it is. It has a kind of sugar in it. Tiny little plants called bacteria live in milk and feed on the sugar. These bacteria are so tiny that you can see them only with a microscope. And like other plants they need warmth to grow.

When you leave milk standing in a warm room for a long time, the milk becomes warm and the bacteria grow fast. As they grow they split up and make more bacteria. To begin with, there will probably be just a few bacteria in the milk. But in a very short time there will be hundreds. They will change the sweet sugar into an acid—something that tastes sour like vinegar. The milk will become sour.

But bacteria can't sour cold milk so quickly. And that's why your mother always asks you to put the milk back into the refrigerator after you've filled your glass.

About Things You Use

How does soap help clean you?

Dirt sticks on your hands or legs or face because your skin has oil in it and the oil holds the dirt there. If you use just plain water, some of the dirt washes off. But oil and water don't mix, so the water bounces away from the oil and much of the dirt remains. But if you use soap something different happens. The bubbly soap gets into the oil, breaks it up, loosens it. And then the rushing water carries away the tiny droplets of oil, along with the dirt that clings to them.

Why do rubbers keep your feet dry?

Water leaks through the cotton and woolen things you wear, because these materials are woven. They have many tiny holes in them, and water gets through the holes. But rubber is not woven. It's a very solid substance with no holes for water to leak through.

Rubber is also stretchy. You stretch your rubbers to get them over your shoes, and then they shrink back into shape. They fit tight. The tightness helps keep water out, too. It helps keep your feet warm and dry.

What makes a ball bounce?

Air—the same kind of air you breathe—makes your ball bounce. The air is trapped inside your ball. When you bounce it on the floor, the bottom of your ball is pushed in. This squeezes the air inside. But right away the squeezed air pushes back against the floor. And this makes your ball bounce back up.

Of course, your ball also bounces because it is made of rubber. Rubber is elastic. It gets pushed out of shape easily but snaps right back.

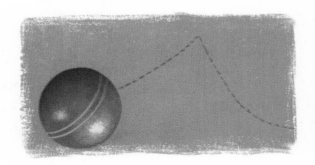

Why do roller skates have ball bearings?

You push a ball across the floor and it rolls along easily and quickly. But if you push a flat box across the floor, it will move much more slowly than the ball. That's because the whole flat side of the box rubs against the floor. And rubbing slows up moving things. In contrast, only a very small part of something round rubs against the floor.

The wheels of your roller skates turn on an axle. If the wheel rubs against this axle it will slow down — just as the box slowed down when it rubbed against the floor. But small steel balls, called ball bearings, are often placed between the wheel and the axle. As the wheel spins around it touches the ball bearings, and they roll against the axle. The wheel is slowed down scarcely at all by rubbing.

Do your skates have ball bearings? You can't see them, but try turning your skate upside down and spinning one wheel. If you hear a clicking sound you will know the skate has ball bearings. These little steel balls hit each other as the wheel turns. And the wheel of a ball-bearing skate always turns faster and spins longer than a simple wheel.

Why does the key fit only the lock of your door?

The key to your door may seem to look like the key to your friend's door. But if you examine them carefully you see that their jagged edges are quite different. When you slip your key into your lock, the little peaks and dips fit exactly into the dips and peaks inside your lock. They were made for each other. Your key is something like a piece of a puzzle. It must fit exactly. When it does, it can turn the moving part inside your lock that locks or unlocks your door.

There are many, many different patterns for keys and locks. Somewhere in the world someone will probably have the same pattern you have, but it isn't very likely that he'll ever find your door.

How can you see yourself in a mirror?

Light streams everywhere. It can go right through a glass window. But it can't shine through you, can it? When light reaches you, it bounces off.

Light does the same thing on a mirror. Most mirrors are made of a pane of glass with a silvery coating on the back. The light cannot pass through this silvery coating. It bounces back, it reflects. When you stand in front of a mirror the light streams from you to the mirror and from the mirror back to you. You see your reflection.

Stand in front of a mirror and raise your right hand. Your reflection or image seems to be raising its left hand. You will find that your reflected image will always be reversed in the mirror.

You can see your reflection in a clear pool of water, too, but it will look wiggly. The ripples on the water will make the light bounce back unevenly. Your mirror is smooth and bright and you will see yourself evenly and clearly.

How does the thermometer work?

That colored or silver line in the middle of the thermometer tells you what the temperature is. In the summer it's a tall line that runs up to the high numbers. In the winter it's a short line ending beside the low numbers.

What is this line that grows tall in hot weather and shrinks in cold weather? Sometimes it is colored alcohol, but more often it's a metallic liquid called mercury. Both mercury and alcohol grow bigger when heat reaches them and both mercury and alcohol grow smaller when cold reaches them. In the narrow glass tube they have no place to go but up when they grow and no place to go but down when they shrink. So we place numbers alongside the tube and measure the height to get the temperature. Convenient, isn't it?

The temperature scale most commonly used on our everyday thermometers is called the *Fahrenheit* scale, after Gabriel D. Fahrenheit, a German physicist who in 1714 built a mercury thermometer of the type used today.

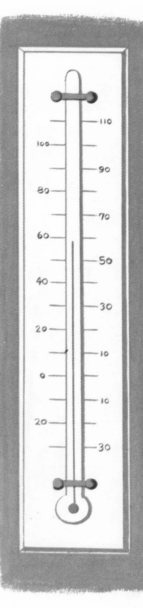

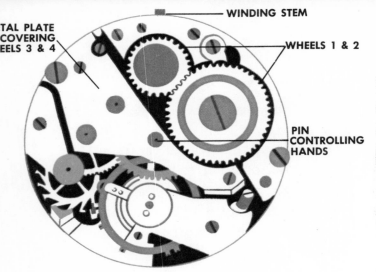

Inside the watch. The winding spring is beneath wheel number 2.

What makes the hands of a watch move?

Inside your watch there is a coil of wire. It is called a spring because it's a springy kind of wire. When you wind your watch, you turn two wheels. They wind the spring into a small, round, tight coil. But it won't stay that way. As soon as you stop winding, the spring slowly begins to push open, to unwind. As it unwinds it starts a third wheel turning. This wheel has teeth which fit into another wheel with teeth.

Wheel number three makes wheel number four start turning. The two wheels push each other round and round.

They are fastened to the hands of the watch and so—what happens? The hands move, too. The spring keeps unwinding. The wheels keep turning. The hands keep moving...until finally the spring is completely unwound. Then everything stops moving, and it's time for you to wind your watch again.

What shuts off an alarm clock?

First, what makes an alarm clock ring? You wind the alarm key just the way you wind the key that keeps the clock going. This tightens a fine wire coil inside, pressing the coil into a tight little circle. This coil is the alarm spring.

Next you set the alarm hand at the time you wish to be waked, and you pull out the small alarm knob. When the hands of your clock match the time of your alarm hand, a tiny rod bumps into the tight alarm spring. It bumps into the spring and starts it unwinding. As the spring unwinds, it presses against a clapper or buzzer and your clock begins to ring or to buzz. How long will it ring? As long as you let it, or until the alarm spring has finished unwinding and no longer presses against the clapper.

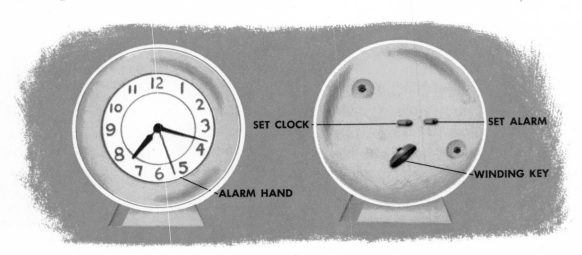

How does a
magnetic can opener work?

A magnetic can opener cuts off the top of the can like any other can opener. But then it does something more. It lifts up the top and holds it. As you probably know, a magnet is doing this, but what is a magnet and how does it work?

A magnet is a piece of metal that has a very special power. It can pull things with iron or steel in them toward itself, and it can hang on to them. Most cans are made of iron or steel coated with another metal such as tin. And so the magnet in the magnetic can opener pulls up the cut-off top and holds it fast.

Some pieces of iron are natural magnets. They are already magnets when found in the earth. But most iron has to be magnetized. One easy way of doing this is to rub the iron against a magnet.

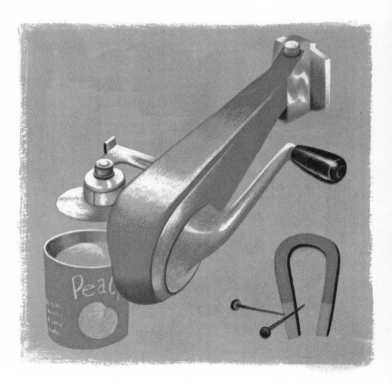

How does your
bathroom scale work?

Your bathroom scale has a spring inside. When you step on the scale the weight of your body presses down on the spring, makes it stretch. The spring is connected to the pointer. It pushes the pointer along a row of numbers which will tell you how many pounds you weigh. How much the spring stretches depends on how heavy you are. You will make it stretch some. Your mother and father will make it stretch more. And the pointer will tell all of you how much you weigh.

Where does electricity come from?

Electricity for your house comes to you from a big power station. In the power station there is a huge piece of machinery called a generator. And inside the generator is an electromagnet. This is an iron core with wires which coil around it but do not touch it.

In a circle around the magnet—but also not touching it—there are other coils of wire. Power, usually from steam or falling water, makes the electromagnet whirl rapidly inside the coil. And this produces electricity, electric current in the outer circle of wire.

The electric current flows from the generator into cables that run sometimes underground and sometimes high up on poles. They carry the current everywhere it is needed. A special cable brings it into your house. When you flip a light switch or turn on your television set, you bring the electric current into your room.

What does a fuse do?

A fuse is small but important, for it helps protect your house from fire. It is the bridge over which all electric current from outside your house travels to the

GENERATORS

POWER STATION

HOME

Two kinds of fuses

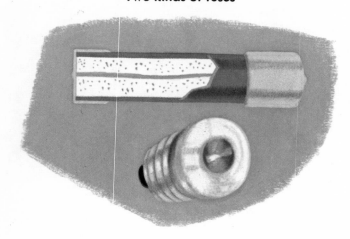

wires inside your house. If you take out the fuse, no current flows in. If you put the fuse back, you have current again.

Inside the fuse there is a piece of metal. It's a special kind of metal that melts very quickly when it becomes too hot. And by melting it protects your house. If too much electricity flows over the wires, they will get very hot and perhaps start a fire. However, before this can happen, the metal piece in the fuse melts from the heat. When this bridge is destroyed, no more current can flow into the wires. And this keeps a fire from starting.

CABLES

the outlet through the second wire and second prong. The current travels around and around and around this path all the time you have your lamp burning.

But sometimes something happens to send the current on a shorter route. The rubber covering on the wires may wear out or tear. The two wires may touch. When the current reaches this place, it crosses over and turns back. It no longer makes the long circuit to your lamp. It takes a short cut called a short circuit. Your lamp no longer lights — even with a new bulb.

How does a light switch work?

Inside your walls, hidden from your eyes, are wires that carry electricity to make lights shine. The electricity is always there waiting to be used. When you flip up or push the switch, you move a small piece of metal inside. This metal makes a bridge between the two ends of a wire. Over this bridge electricity now can flow to your light. When you flip the switch down, the metal piece moves away from the ends of the wire. It separates them. There is no bridge for the electricity to flow over. No electricity, no light!

What is a short circuit?

Circuit is a word something like circle. It means traveling around in a circle. And that's what all electric current does. It travels in a circle. Take a look at the plug of your lamp. There are two prongs at the end of it. These prongs are the ends of two separate wires hidden inside the cord. Each wire is wrapped in a rubber covering to keep it separate.

The current flows from the outlet through one prong, up one wire, into the bulb. The bulb shines. But the current doesn't stop there. It flows back to

What makes the doorbell ring?

You press the button outside the door and inside the house a bell rings. What makes this happen?

Electric current, flowing through a wire, makes the doorbell ring. But unless you press the button, this electric current cannot reach the bellbox inside the house. It cannot reach the bellbox because there is a break or gap in the wire near the button. The current cannot flow through this break.

When you press the button, however, the break between the two ends of the wire is closed. The current flows through a coil of wire around a small piece of iron, the electromagnet inside the bellbox. The electromagnet pulls the bell clapper toward it and lets it go. Back and forth, back and forth the clapper goes. It strikes the bell. The bell rings. It will keep on ringing until you take your finger off the button and stop the flow of electricity over the wire.

Why do some things get rusty?

Do you know what kinds of things get rusty? Perhaps you found out sometime if you left a shovel or a rake on the grass overnight. When you picked them up a few days later, you saw rough, brown spots of rust. Indoors they never got rusty, did they?

Air is made up partly of something called oxygen. This oxygen combines with iron to make rust. And moisture or water helps to bring about the change. Tools such as rakes and shovels are made of iron. And so they rust quickly if they are left out in wet or damp air. If you left them out long enough, they would rust completely and crumble away.

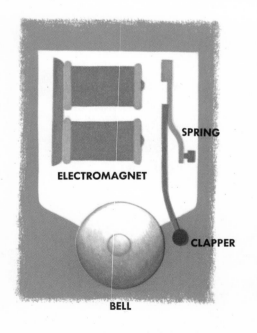

SPRING

ELECTROMAGNET

CLAPPER

BELL

HOW THE BELLBOX LOOKS INSIDE

PUSH BUTTON

BELLBOX

How does your flashlight light up?

The bulb in your flashlight looks like the bigger one in your lamp. It lights up like it, too. But where is the electricity? There's no plug, no wiring.

A cell or a battery of cells inside your flashlight makes electricity and sends it to the bulb. The metal case of the flashlight acts as its wiring. A spring beneath the cell connects the cell to the metal case. When you push the switch you close a little gap between the case and the reflector holding the bulb. Once this gap is closed, then bulb, cell, spring and case are all connected. The light shines brightly.

There is a chemical paste in the cell to help make the electricity. But it has a short life. So when the chemicals in this paste change, the cell no longer makes electricity. We say the cell, or battery, is dead.

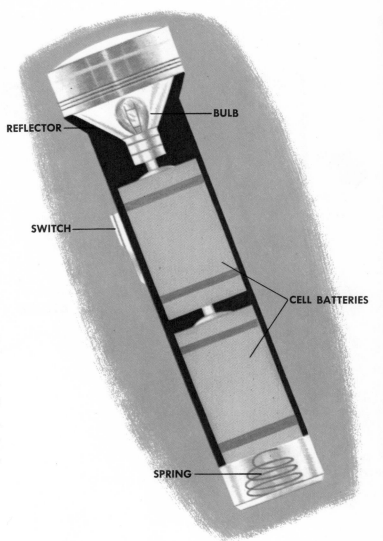

How is paint made?

Red, blue, yellow, brown—all the lovely colors of paint—where do they come from and how do they get into paint?

Color comes from many different kinds of things and places. It comes from the earth, from the sea, from plants, from animals. Dark blue comes from an ore in the earth. And reddish brown comes from a fluid made by a cuttlefish. The color is gotten out and made into a powder. At the paint factory the powder is mixed with a small amount of liquid until it becomes a paste. The liquid may contain oil, water, varnish or rubber.

Grinding machines grind the paste up very fine. And now two fluids are added to it. One thins it out, so that it can be sprayed or spread over a surface with a brush. The other fluid is something that will make the paint dry in the air after it has been used. The mixture now goes to a big whirling machine that mixes the color through it evenly. And then it is paint ready to be poured into big and small cans for use by the painter.

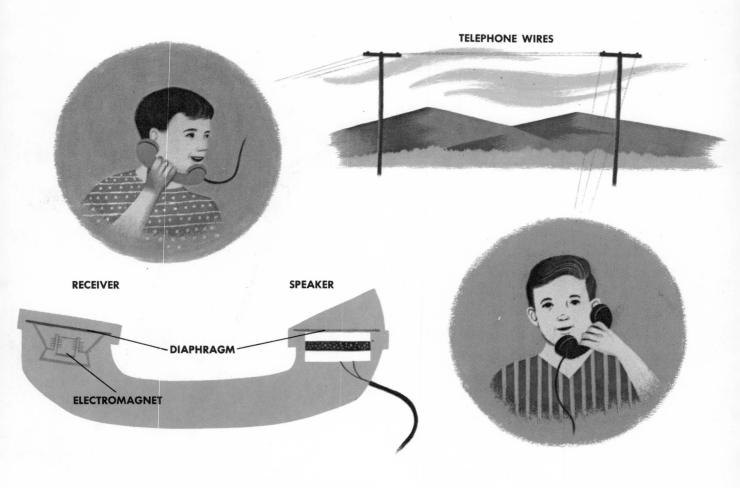

TELEPHONE WIRES

RECEIVER SPEAKER

DIAPHRAGM

ELECTROMAGNET

How does a telephone work?

Every time people talk, they start sound waves moving through the air. When you talk to your friend over the telephone, the sound waves from your voice enter the mouthpiece. They flow against a paper-thin piece of metal called a *diaphragm*. They make it move back and forth, they make it vibrate.

An electric current flows over the telephone wires between your house and your friend's house. As the thin piece of metal in the mouthpiece vibrates, it opens and closes a gap between two telephone wires. This changes the amount of electric current that goes over the wires. It makes the current travel in spurts—sometimes weak, sometimes strong. These spurts follow the same pattern as the sound waves from your voice.

When the spurts of electricity reach your friend's house, they must be changed back into the sound of your voice for your friend to hear. In his phone is a piece of iron with a coil of wire around it. It is called an electromagnet. When the spurts of electricity reach the electromagnet, a thin metal piece or diaphragm in your friend's phone begins to vibrate. These vibrations set sound waves in motion. The sound waves reach your friend's ears and he hears your "hello."

54

How is a record made?

In a recording studio a musician stands in front of a microphone and sings or plays an instrument. All sounds start waves rippling out into the air. And the music he makes sends sound waves to the microphone, to the electrical wiring inside the microphone. The sound waves reach this wiring and are changed into spurts of electricity.

These spurts of electricity are greatly increased in amplifying tubes. Then they travel along to a machine that looks something like your phonograph. It has a turntable and an arm with a needle. But the needle is quite different from the needle on your phonograph. It's a cutting needle with a very sharp point.

And the record disk is quite different from the records you play. It has no grooves, and it's made of a special kind of material that can be cut easily and cleanly. This disk turns around under the needle just as the record spins around on your phonograph.

As the needle cuts a groove into the disk, the spurts of electricity make the needle quiver and vibrate. The groove it cuts is uneven, wavy. It ripples in the same way the sound waves from the music rippled out into the air. This is how the master record is made, and many more copies will be made from it so that you and thousands like you can have the music to play in your home whenever you like.

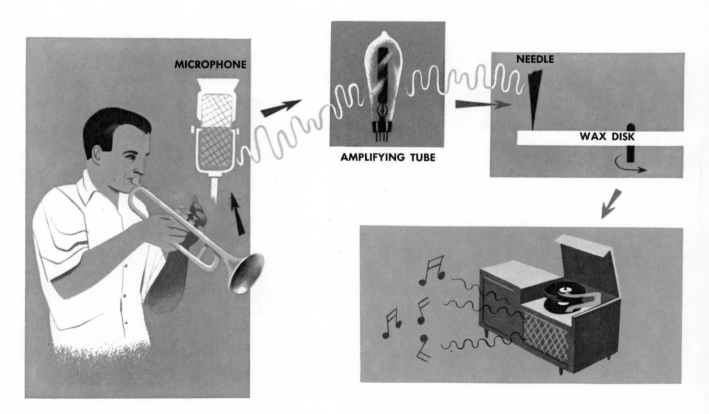

Musician in recording studio

Finished record turning on the phonograph

How does your phonograph work?

The record spins. You listen, and you hear music. You watch, and what do you see? You see the record spinning around and around and around under the needle. The needle fits down into the groove, stays there while the groove passes under it.

This groove is not a smooth path for the needle. It is full of tiny bumps, wiggles and waves. You can see that this is true if you look carefully at the moving needle. It keeps jiggling, vibrating. The groove is uneven because it was made by uneven vibrations, vibrations that began as sound waves in the studio.

The vibrations of the needle pass through it to the wiring in the arm of the phonograph. There they become spurts of electricity and move along to the loud-speaker. When the spurts of electricity reach the loud-speaker, a small piece of metal in the speaker vibrates, the electrical spurts are turned into sound waves, the same pattern of sound waves that once filled the studio. These sound waves roll out into the room to your ears, and you hear music.

How does your camera work?

When you click your camera you open a shutter in front of a glass lens. You let light inside. It flashes back to your film. Your film has been chemically treated so that a bright light makes a black patch on it and a dim light makes a pale gray patch. Your father's white shirt will make a dark patch, for a great deal of light bounces off anything white. Your mother's black dress will make a pale gray patch, because very little light bounces off black.

When your film is developed—that is, when you have a negative—you will see your father in a black shirt and your mother in a white dress. That's all wrong, isn't it? But just wait, the next step will correct that. The negative will be placed on a special kind of paper under a bright light. Not much light will shine through your father's black shirt and so on the paper it will print white. A great deal of light will shine through your mother's gray dress and it will print black. And that's exactly right, isn't it?

GLASS-PRESSING MACHINE WITH MOLDS

GLASS ARTIST SHAPING GLASS

HOT GLASS BEING PUT INTO MOLD

How is glass made?

When you look at shiny glass, when you feel how smooth it is, you can hardly believe that it is made of three grainy, powdery things. But it is. Finely ground sand, baking soda and chalky limestone are mixed together in a big vat. They are cooked over a very hot furnace until they melt and become a liquid. This is liquid glass, ready now to be shaped, cooled and left to harden.

Huge machines with blowers blow the liquid glass into molds to become glasses, bowls, vases, plates. Or they blow it out flat under rollers to make window panes. There are still a few "glass artists" today who blow glass the way people used to years ago. They blow into a blob of liquid glass through a long tube. Their breath shapes the glass. What they make is a work of art. But machines do a good enough job for our everyday glass things.

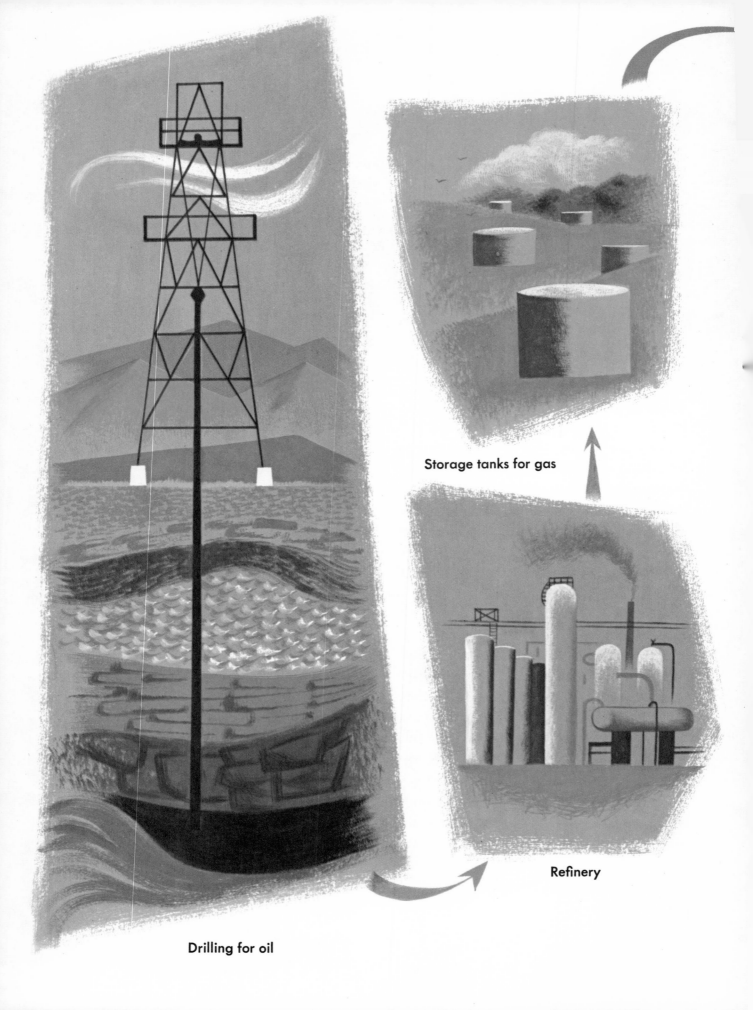

Storage tanks for gas

Refinery

Drilling for oil

Transporting gas

How does gasoline get to the gas station?

Gasoline to make our cars run comes from the earth. It comes from the oil that men drill deep into the earth to find. This oil is piped to a plant called a refinery. There it is separated into many different kinds of useful products. And one of the most useful products is gasoline.

The gasoline is piped into huge storage tanks near the refinery. Here tank trucks, seagoing tankers and railway tank cars come to load up. They carry the gasoline to local storage places all over the country, and even all over the world. At the local storage tanks, the gas delivery men fill up their tank trucks and go off to service the gas stations on their routes. It is the job of these delivery men to keep the tanks underneath the gas pumps filled with gasoline for the many cars that pull in for gas.

Gas station

How is paper made?

The paper in this book was once part of a tree, for most paper is made of wood. Tiny slivers of wood are tossed into a vat of chemicals and left to soak. The chemicals soften them, bleach or whiten them, and make them stick together.

After a while there is a wet sticky mass inside the vat. This is paper pulp.

As the pulp flows in a thin layer over a fine mesh, water drips out of it. Carried along on a moving belt, it passes between heavy warm rollers. They press out more water and make it dry. As soon as it's dry, it's paper.

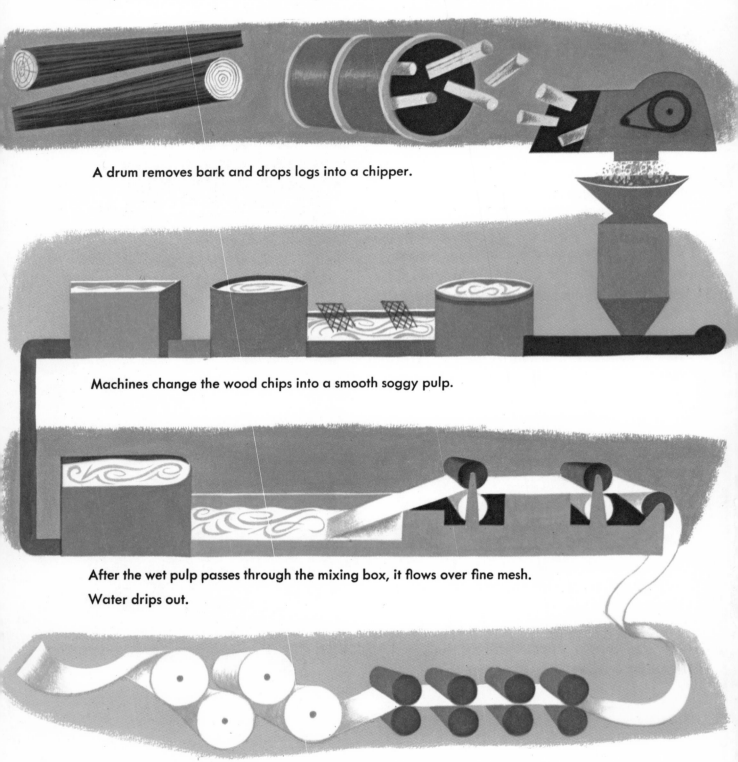

A drum removes bark and drops logs into a chipper.

Machines change the wood chips into a smooth soggy pulp.

After the wet pulp passes through the mixing box, it flows over fine mesh.
Water drips out.

Finally rollers and heat press and dry the pulp into rolls of thin paper.

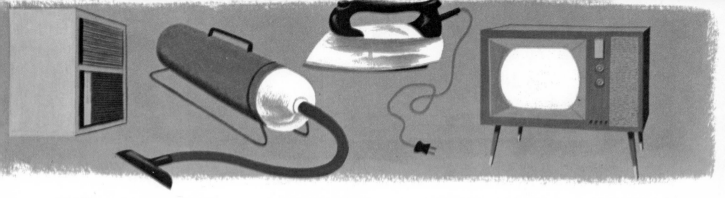

About Machines That Work For You

How does a washing machine work?

Your mother tosses the dirty clothes into the machine. She plugs it into the electric outlet. She presses a button and walks away. The electric motor does what her muscles would have had to do in the days before the electric washing machine was invented. And the timer does the brain work.

The timer is a round dial that marks off the number of minutes needed for each job. It turns, and as it turns it opens and closes electrical switches. Notches on the timer meet up with each switch at just the right minute. First the timer pushes the switch that pulls the stopper away from the water hose. Water rushes into the tub. Then at just the right minute the timer meets the next switch that pushes the stopper back in. And at just the right minute it pushes the switch that makes the inside drum whirl or starts an agitator beating. The clothes whirl and slap together in the foamy water.

At just the right minute the timer pushes the switch to stop the whirling or beating. And then it meets up with the switch that opens up the drain pipe to let the dirty water out. The timer keeps turning and meeting all the switches that are needed to wash, rinse, and finally to whirl the clothes and fling out the water.

Last of all it pushes the switch that shuts off the motor. The wash is finished.

TIMER

How does a drier work?

What makes clothes flapping on a clothesline get dry? The wind blowing against the clothes shakes some of the water out, and heat from the sun does the rest. An electric drier dries clothes in much the same way. It makes its own heat and has its own way of shaking out the water.

Electricity flows into the drier. It is forced through wires that grow red hot, and heats the air around the clothes in the drier. Electricity also starts a motor that makes the clothes whirl inside the drier. They fly around fast, flapping and tumbling. The drops of water are flung out of them and flow away through the drain. If you leave the clothes in the drier long enough they will come out just as dry as if they had been flapping outside on a line.

How does an electric iron stay at the right heat?

Your mother sets her iron at the place marked COTTON. The iron gets just so hot. It doesn't get much cooler and it doesn't get any hotter. Something inside her iron—something called a thermostat—keeps the heat even.

The thermostat controls the heat by stopping and starting the electric current. It is made of two strips of metal, usually brass and steel, fastened or welded together. When the iron gets

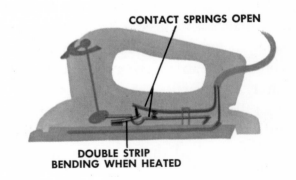

CONTACT SPRINGS OPEN

DOUBLE STRIP
BENDING WHEN HEATED

hot both metals get hot, too. Heat makes them both stretch or expand, but the brass strip stretches more than the steel one.

However, the brass strip cannot just stretch out by itself, for it is fastened to the steel strip. Instead, the double strip bends. As it bends it pushes the contact springs open, making a gap in the wiring. Electric current stops flowing into the iron. With the current off, the brass strip cools and shrinks back until it is no longer pressing against the contact springs. At once the gap is closed. Current to heat the iron flows again.

Your mother's iron is being turned on and off continually by the thermostat, and this keeps the heat quite even.

What makes the refrigerator cold?

Have you ever noticed how cool your wet hand feels when you hold it out in the air? The heat from your hand changes the water on it to vapor. The air carries off the vapor and along with it goes some of the heat from your hand. Something like this happens inside your electric refrigerator. But instead of warm water, the refrigerator uses a chemical called Freon to do the cooling.

Freon starts out as a liquid at the bottom of your refrigerator. A pump pushes it up through a pipe which coils around the freezing compartment. And here the cooling action begins. The Freon turns to vapor and takes up the heat from inside the compartment. At once the coils begin to grow cold. The

freezing compartment begins to grow cold. The whole refrigerator begins to grow cold.

The pump then sucks the Freon vapor back down and forces it into a much smaller pipe. This squeezes the Freon vapor and changes it back into a liquid. The heat leaves the Freon, passing into the air outside the refrigerator. By the time the liquid Freon reaches the bottom of the refrigerator, it is ready for another cooling trip.

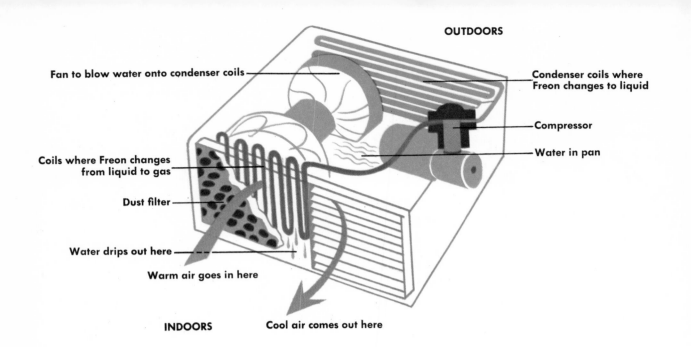

OUTDOORS

Fan to blow water onto condenser coils

Condenser coils where Freon changes to liquid

Compressor

Water in pan

Coils where Freon changes from liquid to gas

Dust filter

Water drips out here

Warm air goes in here

INDOORS

Cool air comes out here

How does an air conditioner work?

An air conditioner is a kind of refrigerator, isn't it? It cools the air, and the air cools the people in a room in the same way food is cooled inside your refrigerator. And air conditioners, like refrigerators, often use Freon to do the job.

The Freon starts out as a liquid inside the coils of the air conditioner. A fan blows the warm moist air from the room over these coils. The Freon is changed to vapor and this vapor takes up the heat in the warm air. This cools the coils in the same way that perspiration turning to vapor cools you. The coils grow cold.

The air over them grows cold. Water drips out of the air into a pan, because cold air cannot hold as much water as warm air. The air over the coils becomes cool and dry, and a fan blows this cool dry air into the room, cooling both the room and everyone in it.

Meanwhile the water in the pan is blown onto a second set of coils—the hot condenser coils. These coils evaporate the water into the air outside the house. The Freon vapor is sucked back down by a pump. It is squeezed very hard in the compressor and changed back to a liquid. This makes it ready for a return trip up to the coils.

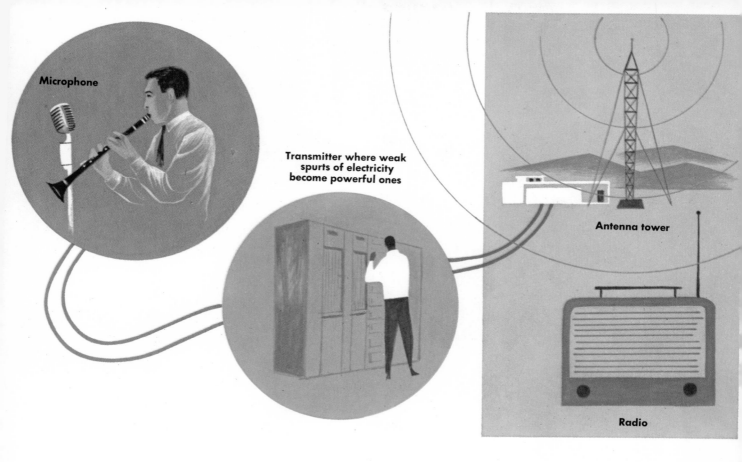

Microphone

Transmitter where weak
spurts of electricity
become powerful ones

Antenna tower

Radio

How does a radio work?

How does music come to your radio? There are no wires as there are in your telephone to carry sounds to you from far away. There is no record such as you have in your phonograph. The music just seems to come out of the air. How does this happen?

In a broadcasting studio a musician is playing or singing before a microphone. The sounds he makes set waves moving through the air. Some of these sound waves strike the microphone and are changed into spurts or waves of electricity. These electrical waves go on wires to a place where they are strengthened and changed into radio waves that can travel long distances. The radio waves are then fed into the broadcasting

antenna, usually a tower reaching high into the air. From up there they spread out into space in all directions.

Every station has its own pattern of waves, its own wave length. You have only to turn the dial on your radio and tune in on the station you want. The antenna in your radio will catch the right wave length. The radio waves will start an electrical current in your antenna. And then they will be turned back into electrical waves like the ones that were made in the microphone at the broadcasting studio. The loud-speaker in your radio will change these electrical waves back to sound waves. As sound waves they will ripple out into your room. And your ears will hear them as music—the same music the musician is making in the broadcasting studio.

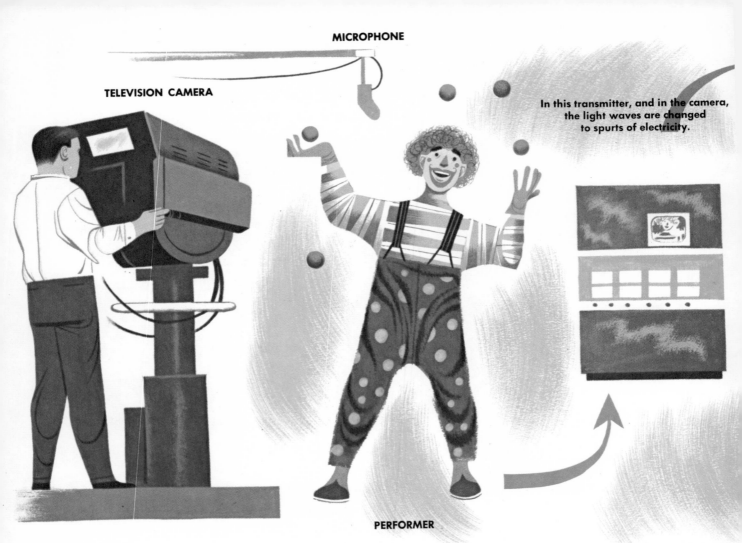

TELEVISION CAMERA

MICROPHONE

In this transmitter, and in the camera, the light waves are changed to spurts of electricity.

PERFORMER

How does television work?

Somewhere far off in a television studio someone is putting on a show. At almost the same moment you see it on the television set in your own home. How can this possibly happen?

A kind of motion picture camera with a very special sort of screen performs this magic. In an ordinary motion picture camera the light flashes through the lens to a film and prints a pattern of dark and light. But with a television camera the light flashes back to a screen that has been treated with a special chemical. The light reaches the screen and changes to electricity.

Bright light becomes strong spurts of electricity. Dim light becomes weak spurts. There is an electrical picture of the show on the special screen inside the camera. The spurts or waves of electricity are turned into stronger waves that can spread out into space from a high television antenna.

At the same time a microphone is

A high antenna sends out electromagnetic television waves.

On the television screen the electrical waves are turned back into light waves.

What makes the candy drop out of the candy machine?

You slip your coin in the slot. You pull the knob. And there's your candy. Your coin does this job. But just what does it do?

The coin drops down a chute to a spring inside the machine. There the coin bounces down on the spring and jars it. The spring is connected to a little trap door that holds up the candy. When your coin jars the spring, the spring jerks open the little trap door. And the candy drops through. By the time you've picked it up, the spring has already closed the trap door again. You will have to put in another coin to open it.

picking up the sound waves. These sound waves will be changed into electrical waves that will travel alongside the waves from the picture. You turn on your television set and your antenna catches both sets of waves, bringing them into your television set. The electrical waves from the camera are turned into light waves. They make a black-and-white picture on the screen of your television set. The other set of waves comes out of your loud-speaker as sound waves. You see and hear the show.

How does the toaster work?

You know that it's electricity that makes your toaster toast bread, but how does the current get there? And what exactly does it do?

You bring the electric current to the toaster when you plug the cord into the outlet. The two prongs at the end of the plug are fastened to wires that run to the toaster. The current flows through the wires. You bring the current inside the toaster when you press down the bar to turn it on. Now the current reaches the wires inside.

These inside wires are made of a special mixture of metals. Electricity cannot pass through them easily. They hold up the current. As the electricity is forced through, it makes the wires grow hot, very hot. You can see them turn red and glowing. It's the heat from these wires that changes soft white bread to crisp brown toast.

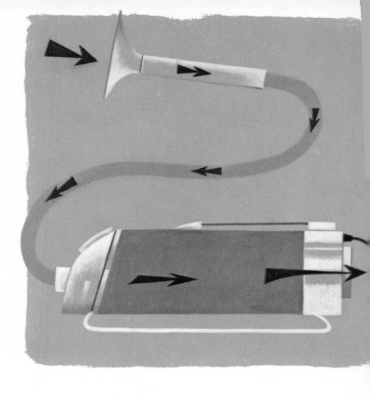

How does the vacuum cleaner work?

The vacuum cleaner sucks up the dirt so fast. How does it do it? First, of course, you plug your vacuum into the outlet to make a path for the electricity to flow from the wires behind the wall into the motor of the cleaner. You press the switch and whir! The motor starts a small fan whirling. As the fan whirls it stirs up the air inside the cleaner, pushes it out through the back opening. You can feel the air being pushed out at the back when you put your hand there.

Now the outside air from the front rushes in to fill the empty space. You can feel this rush of air, too, by putting your hand over the nozzle. Dirt, crumbs, shreds of paper—all are carried in by the rushing air. They are trapped in the bag. And there they stay while air keeps rushing in and through the vacuum cleaner like a strong breeze.

Index

Air, 9, 12, 13, 14, 15, 17, 20, 21, 22, 24, 26, 29, 40, 41, 45, 52, 54, 55, 63, 64, 68
Air conditioners, 64
Alarm clocks, 48
Alcohol,
    in thermometers, 47
Amplifying tubes, 55
Antenna, 65, 66-67
Apples
    dark spots on, 44
    worms in, 44

Babies, walking and, 32
Bacteria, see also Germs, 40, 42, 43, 44
Baking powder, 40
Baking soda, 57
Ball bearings, 46
Balls, bouncing, 45
Batteries, 53
Bells, electric, 52
Blinking, 31
Blood, 29, 33, 34
Body, the, 27-34
    cells of, 27, 28, 31, 32, 33
    growth of, 27
    heat of, 26
    nerves of, 28, 29
    strength, 27-28
Boilers, 23
Bones, development of, 32
Booster shots, 34
Brain, 28, 29
Bread, 37
Breath, seeing,
    on cold days, 20
Broadcasting, 65
Bubbles
    gas, 37, 40
    in boiling water, 26
Butter, 40
Butter milk, 40

Cacao tree, 35-36
Cakes, 40
Cameras, 56, 66-67
Can opener, magnetic, 49
Candy machines, 67
Cans, food in, 42
Cavities, in teeth, 30
Cells
    in body, 27, 28, 31, 32, 33
    in flashlight, 53
    in fruit, 44
Chocolate, 35-36, 41
Churns, 40
Circuit, short, 50-51
Circulatory system, 29
Clocks, alarm, 48
Clothes driers, electric, 62
Clothing, warmth of, 26
Clouds 12, 13, 14, 15

Coal, 22, 24
Cocoa, 35
Color
    in paint, 53
    rainbow, 13
    skin, 32
    sky, 9
Cooking-pots, metal, 25
Cooling pipes, 41
Coughs, 33
Cream, 39, 40, 41
Current, electric, 50-52, 54, 62, 63, 65, 68

Day, 9
Dew, 15
Diaphragm, 54
Digestive system, 28
Diphtheria, 34
Diseases, 33, 34
Doorbells, 52
Drain pipes, 19, 61
Driers, clothes, 62
Dust particles, 9, 12, 31

Earth, the, 10, 12, 13, 14, 15, 16, 35, 53, 59
    rotation of, 9
Electricity, 14, 42, 50-56, 61, 62, 65, 66, 68
Electromagnet, 50, 52, 54
Enamel, of teeth, 30
Eyes, blinking of, 31

Fahrenheit scale, 47
Faucets, 18, 19
Film, camera, 56
Fingernails, 29
Fire, 21-25, 35, 50
Flashlights, 53
Flour, 36
Food, 25, 26, 27, 35-44
    bacteria and, 40, 42, 43
    canned, 42
    fresh, 42, 43
    frozen, 43
    growth of body and, 27
    strength and, 27-28
    taste of, 31
    teeth and, 30
Freckles, 32
Freon, 63, 64
Frozen foods, 43
Fruit, 44
Furnaces, 22-23
Fuses, 50

Gas, 11, 23-24, 37, 40
Gasoline, 59
Gelatin, 41
Generator, 50
Germs, see also Bacteria, 33, 39, 40, 42
Glass
    cold, "sweat" on, 17

cracked by heat, 24, 25
    making of, 57
Goose flesh, 32
Grass, 15
Gravity, 9
Growth, cause of, 27

Hair, 29, 32
Heart, 29, 30
Heat, 21-26, 41, 62
    body, 26
    thermostats and, 62-63
Hopper, 37

Ice, 15, 17, 42
Ice cream, 41
Insects, 44
Intestines, 28
Irons, electric, 62
Islands, 16

Keys, 46

Light
    cameras and, 56
    reflected, 10, 47
    sun, 9, 10, 11, 13
Light switch, 50, 51
Light waves, 66-67
Lightning, 14
Limestone, used in making glass, 57
Locks, 46
Loud-speakers, 56, 65, 67
Lungs, 30

Machines, 61-68
Magnet, 49
Matches, 21
Measles, 33
Mercury, in thermometers, 47
Metal pots, heat and, 25
Microphones, 55, 65, 66
Microscope, electron, 33
Milk, 39, 41, 42
    sour, 44
Mirrors, 47
Moon, 10
Motion-picture
    cameras, 66
Mouth, 28, 31
Muscles, 32

Nails, see Fingernails; Toenails
Natural gas, 23
Needle, cutting, in recording machine, 55
Nerves, 28
Nervous system, 28
Night, 9
Nose, 31

Ocean, 16, 17, 35
Oil, 59
Oxygen, 21, 24, 52

Pain, 28, 29
Paint, 53
Paper, 60
Pepper, 35
Petroleum, see Oil
Phonograph
    records, 55, 56
Photographs, 56
Photography, 56, 66-67
Pipes
    cooling, 41
    drain, 19, 61
    gas, 23-24
    milk, 39
    water, 18, 19, 22-23
Polio, 33, 34
Pots, metal, heat and, 25
Pulp, paper, 60
Pumps, 18

Radiators, 22-23
Radios, 65
Rain, 13, 17
Rainbows, 9, 13
Records,
    phonograph, 55, 56
Refineries
    oil, 59
    sugar, 38
Refrigerators, 39, 41, 42, 44, 63, 64
Reservoirs, 18
Roller skates,
    ball bearings in, 46
Rubber, 45, 50
Rust, 52

Salt, 17, 35, 37
Sand, 16, 57
Scabs, 29
Scale
    bathroom, 49
    Fahrenheit, 47
Sea, see Ocean
Serum, 34
Sewers, 19
Shadow, 11
Short circuit, 50-51
Shots, anti-disease, 34
Silver spoons,
    heat and, 25
Skates, ball-bearing, 46
Skin, 29, 32, 34, 45
Sky, 9, 11, 12, 13
Smallpox, 34
Smell, sense of, 31
Smoke, 21
Snow, 15
Soap, cleansing
    action of, 45
Sound waves, 54-56, 65, 67
Sour milk, 44
Space, 11, 65, 66
Spoons, heat and, 25

Spring
    alarm, in clocks, 48
    in bathroom scales, 49
    in slot machines, 67
    watch, 48
Stars, 11
Steam, 23, 26
Stethoscopes, 30
Stomach, 28
Stoves, gas, 23-24, 25
Strength, food and, 27-28
Sugar, 36, 38, 41
    in milk, 44
Sugar cane, 38
Sun, 9, 10, 11, 12, 13, 15, 35, 62
Sunlight, 9, 10, 11, 13
"Sweat" on cold glass, 17
Switch, light, 50, 51

Tank trucks, milk, 39
Taste, 31
Teeth, cavities in, 30
Telephones, 54
Television, 66-67
Thermometers, 47
Thermos, 26, 39
Thermostats, 62-63
Thunder, 14
Timers, on washing machines, 61
Toasters, 68
Toenails, 29
Tongue, taste buds on, 31

Vaccinations, 34
Vacuum, 26
Vacuum cleaners, 68
Vapor, water, 12, 15, 17, 20, 63, 64
Viruses, 33, 34

Walking, 32
Washers, 19
Washing machines, 61
Watches, 48
Water, 12, 13, 15, 16, 17-20, 21
    boiling, 26
    drinking, 17, 18
    hot, 19, 23
    ocean, 16
    reservoirs, 18
    salt, 17
    source of, 18
Water pipes, 18, 19, 22-23
Weather, 12, 13, 14, 15
Wheat, 36
Wind, 14, 62
Windows, steam on, 20
Wood, 60
Worms, in fruit, 44

Yeast, 37

What are the stars?

HOW IS BREAD MADE?

WHAT IS A GERM?

Where does sugar

HOW IS GLASS MADE?

How does a telephone work?

WHAT MAKES CLOUDS? WHAT MAKES IT RAIN?

Why does ice float?

Why is the water in the ocean salty?

WHY DOES SMOKE GO UP?

IF THE EARTH IS ROUND, WHY

HOW DOES YOUR CAMERA WORK?

Why is the sky blue?

What holds an island up?